God's
New Wine

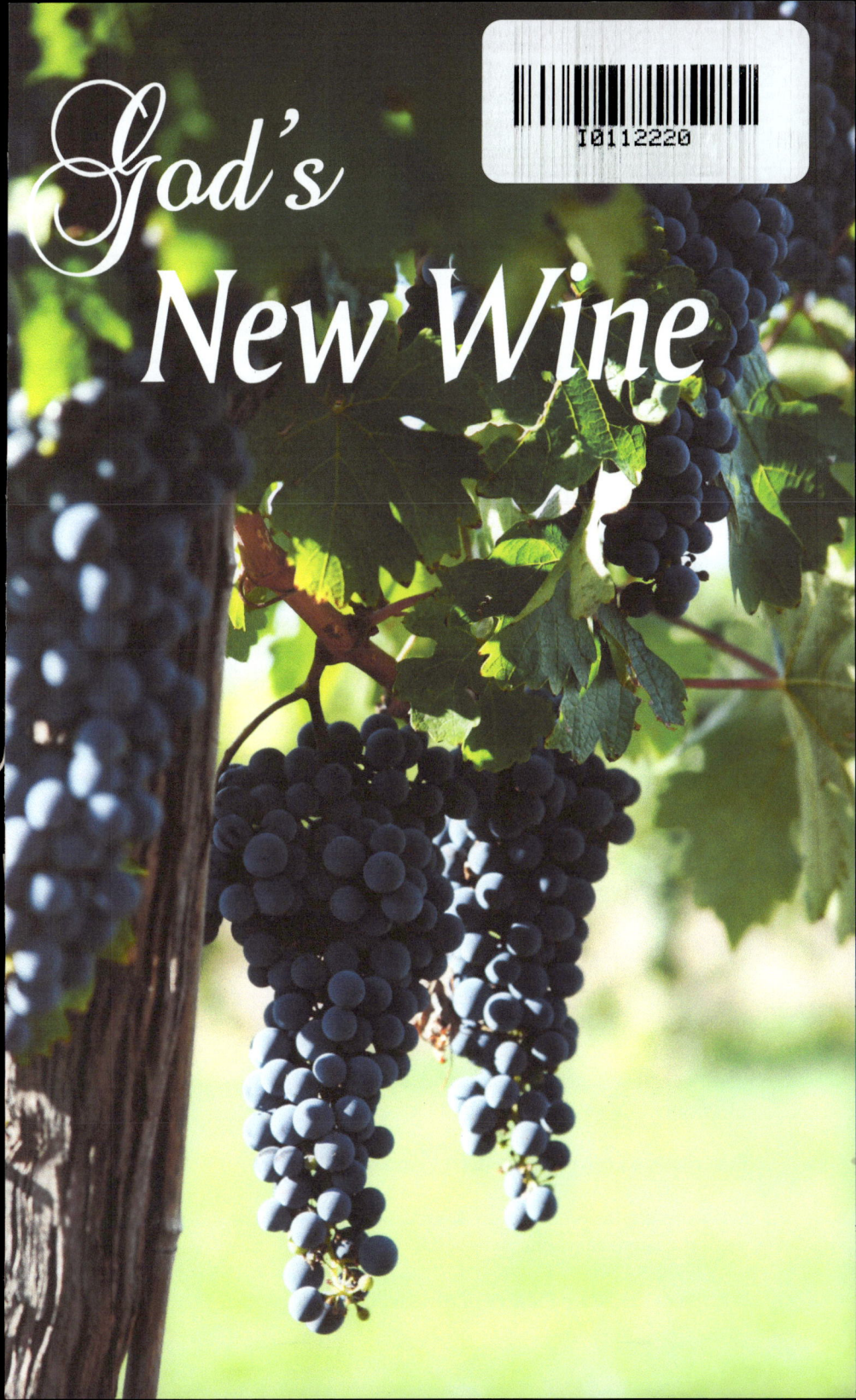

Updated November 2024

GOD'S NEW WINE
Poetic verses by Kathleen Schubitz

Published by:
RPJ & COMPANY, INC.
RPJandco.com
Orlando, Florida, U.S.A.

ISBN-13: 978-1-937770-60-0

Cover and Interior Design: Kathleen Schubitz

Cover Image Copyright © Sherri Camp - Fotolia.com

Scripture quotations from the King James Version of the Bible. Used by permission. All rights reserved.

Printed in the United States of America.

*Dedicated to every believer
who chooses to press on
and never give up!*

*God will do something wonderful
for those who will seek truth and obey.*

*W*alking with Jesus
protects us from sinking;

*H*e delivers us from hell and
wrong thinking.

He offers long life rather than an early death;

He is the giver of life with one simple breath.

*God's Spirit leads us
in a gentle way,*

*Exposing lies that lead
people astray.*

Enlightening and
revealing, God will set
us free,

As we keep our hearts and
eyes fixed on eternity.

$\mathcal{C}$hanging our minds from lies
we believed in childhood,

$\mathcal{W}$e'll refuse to be enticed by
words sounding good.

9

The battle for our souls
can no longer be ignored;

We must hunger for more truth
as never before.

*R*epentance frees us from curses that open the door;

Legal rights that satan once had will be no more.

*Blinded and deceived for
so many a year,*

*We conclude the Lord will no
longer draw near.*

It's a personal choice to walk in godly wisdom,

But Christ followers flee sin to enter His kingdom.

As we journey, our faith
must be in the Lord,

Strongly united with a
heavenly cord.

Prevent the enemy from stealing and being a thief;

Stop agreeing with him; refuse all doubt and unbelief.

*The Holy Spirit reveals
enemy lies as we
trust in Him,*

*Renouncing ungodly spirits
enable us to turn from sin.*

Turning away from evil
and wickedness

Protects us from harm and
unwarranted mess.

Our choices past will be
used to make crooked
things straight,

So believe and trust in Him;
it is never too late.

Binding ourselves to
God's heart, we're able
to see,

While quietly discerning *God's*
voice so clearly.

God gives us power to renounce evil vows and please our King,

Rather than agree with counterfeit spirits and every evil thing.

Alas! With the blinders removed and ears now unplugged,

He reminds us that all things are made new with His love!

*It's time to stop the enemy
from messing inside
our head.*

*God says, I will create a corkscrew
for the new wine instead!*

KATHLEEN SCHUBITZ is an inspired writer and designer. God's spoken word from Romans 14:17 birthed RPJ & Company (Righteousness, Peace and Joy) in 2004, thereby establishing a Kingdom publishing business for God's people. As founder and president, her faith in God and desire to follow His leading compels her to pursue her own writing and publish books, devotionals, greeting cards, calendars and marketing materials for leaders and anointed Kingdom writers.

After growing up in the Midwestern United States, Kathleen presently resides in central Florida. Preparation for her calling comes from serving at Rotary International headquarters as production assistant for *The Rotarian* magazine. Having now become an inspirational writer, she lives a life of dedication to God, choosing to turn life's hardships into stepping stones for success. Pressing through an oppressive childhood, life-threatening abuse and sickness as an adult, Kathleen allows the Spirit of God to turn her tragedies into triumph and devastation into dedication. Victorious over her own hurts and woundedness from the past, she now helps others discover truth to live a life of freedom. Visit: RPJandco.com to learn more.

Scripture verses for further study and reflection:

Genesis 2:7 - And the Lord God formed man of the dust of the ground, and breathed into his nostrils the breath of life; and man became a living soul.

Psalm 58:3 - The wicked are estranged from the womb: they go astray as soon as they be born, speaking lies.

Proverbs 1:10 - My son, if sinners entice thee, consent thou not.

Matthew 5:6 - Blessed are they which do hunger and thirst after righteousness: for they shall be filled.

Matthew 9:13 - But go ye and learn what that meaneth, I will have mercy, and not sacrifice: for I am not come to call the righteous, but sinners to repentance.

Deuteronomy 11:16 - Take heed to yourselves, that your heart be not deceived, and ye turn aside, and serve other gods, and worship them;

Luke 21:8 - And he said, Take heed that ye be not deceived: for many shall come in my name, saying, I am Christ; and the time draweth near: go ye not therefore after them.

Psalm 73:28 - But it is good for me to draw near to God: I have put my trust in the Lord God, that I may declare all thy works.

Matthew 18:3 - And said, Verily I say unto you, Except ye be converted, and become as little children, ye shall not enter into the kingdom of heaven.

Matthew 21:21 - Jesus answered and said unto them, Verily I say unto you, If ye have faith, and doubt not, ye shall not only do this which is done to the fig tree, but also if ye shall say unto this mountain, Be thou removed, and be thou cast into the sea; it shall be done.

Proverbs 29:24 - Whoso is partner with a thief hateth his own soul: he heareth cursing, and bewrayeth it not.

Hebrews 3:19 - So we see that they could not enter in because of unbelief.

Mark 11:23 - For verily I say unto you, That whosoever shall say unto this mountain, Be thou removed, and be thou cast into the sea; and shall not doubt in his heart, but shall believe that those things which he saith shall come to pass; he shall have whatsoever he saith.

Proverbs 3:5 - 5 Trust in the Lord with all thine heart; and lean not unto thine own understanding.

Malachi 3:18 - Then shall ye return, and discern between the righteous and the wicked, between him that serveth God and him that serveth him not.

Revelation 21:5 - And he that sat upon the throne said, Behold, I make all things new. And he said unto me, Write: for these words are true and faithful.

Luke 5:38 - But new wine must be put into new bottles; and both are preserved.

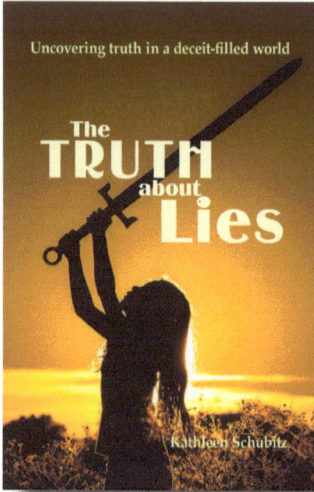
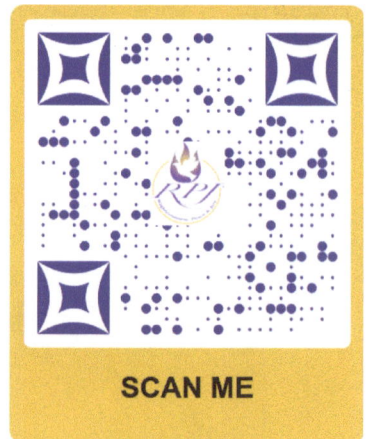

NEW RELEASES IN 2024-25

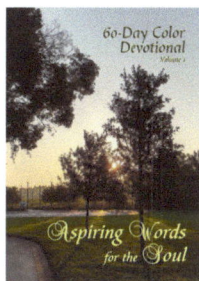

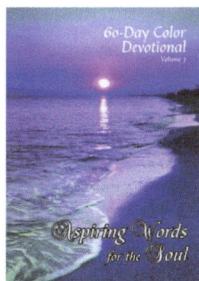

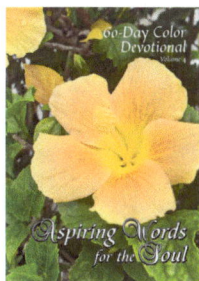

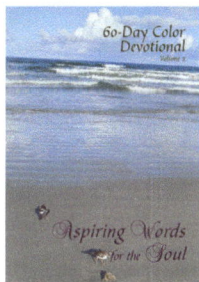

60-Day Color Devotional:
Aspiring Words for the Soul

Pick a favorite color or nature scene. Devotionals available early through RPJ & Company

SCAN ME

Pastor-approved!

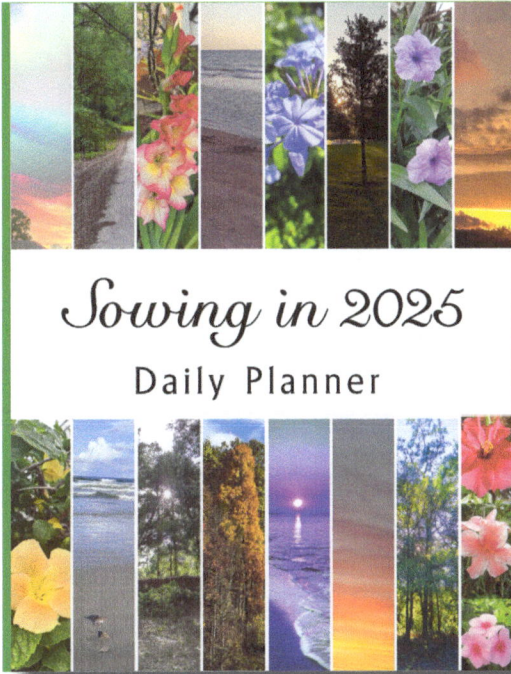

BOOKS BY KATHLEEN SCHUBITZ
Organized by category for easy searching.
Just scan the QR code of choice!

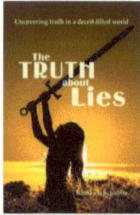

NEW
The Truth about Lies

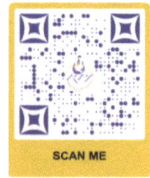

SCAN ME

NEW
60-Day Devotional:
Aspiring Words for the Soul
7 volumes

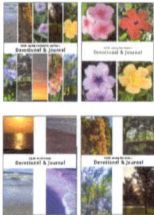

SCAN ME

NEW - Devotional/Journals
S.E.W. during a sunset or sunrise
S.E.W. at the beach
S.E.W. among the trees
S.E.W. among the flowers

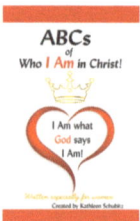

SCAN ME

ABC Books
ABCs of Who I Am in Christ!
ABC Woman finds Freedom
ABC Journal to Freedom

SCAN ME

BOOKS BY KATHLEEN SCHUBITZ
Organized by category for easy searching.
Just scan the QR code of choice!

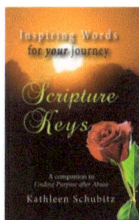

Finding Purpose after Abuse and companion books
Leader's Guide, Journal to Freedom, Scripture Keys, Living with Purpose Journal, Any Time Inspiration for Survivors

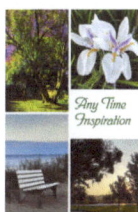

SCAN ME

Devotionals
Any Time Inspiration, Aspiring Words for the Soul, His Heart Calls, Lord, I Praise You, Lord, I Thank You, Accept, Believe and Create

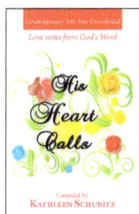

SCAN ME

Journals
His Heart Calls, S.E.W. journals, Journal to Freedom, Living with Purpose Journal, ABC Journal to Freedom, Lord, I Thank You

SCAN ME

Poetry Books
...In His Presence, Any Time Inspiration, God's New Wine, Healing for the Soul, Lord, I Praise You, Lord, I Worship You, Personal Poetic Promises, Poetic Prayers

SCAN ME

SCAN ME

To view all print books by RPJ & Company, Inc.

www.ingramcontent.com/pod-product-compliance
Lightning Source LLC
LaVergne TN
LVHW010029070426
835513LV00001B/31